RODEO CLOWN

BY NICK GORDON

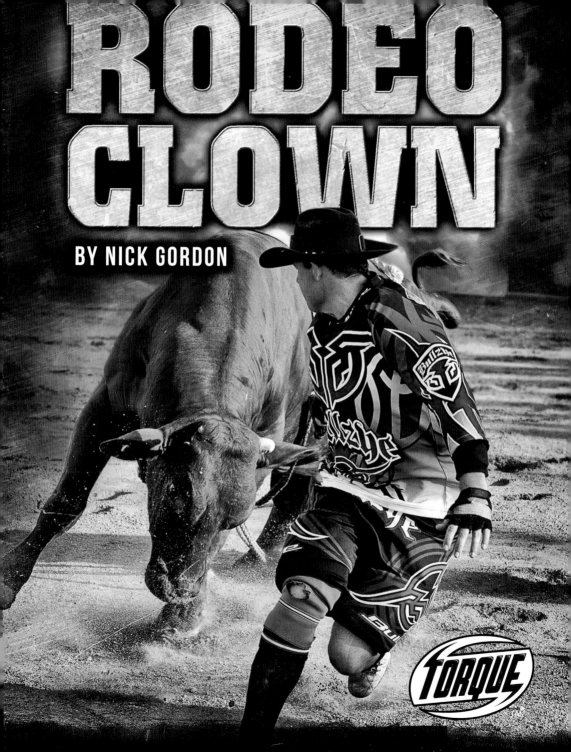

BELLWETHER MEDIA · MINNEAPOLIS, MN

Are you ready to take it to the extreme?
Torque books thrust you into the action-packed world
of sports, vehicles, mystery, and adventure. These books
may include dirt, smoke, fire, and dangerous stunts.
WARNING: read at your own risk.

Library of Congress Cataloging-in-Publication Data

Gordon, Nick.
  Rodeo clown / by Nick Gordon.
     p. cm. -- (Torque: dangerous jobs)
  Includes bibliographical references and index.
  Summary: "Engaging images accompany information about rodeo clowns. The combination
of high-interest subject matter and light text is intended for students in grades 3 through 7"
--Provided by publisher.
  ISBN 978-1-60014-896-5 (hardcover : alk. paper)
  1. Rodeo clowns--Juvenile literature. I. Title.
  GV1834.5.G67 2013
  791.8'4--dc23
                          2012042321

This edition first published in 2013 by Bellwether Media, Inc.

Printed in the United States of America, North Mankato, MN.

TABLE OF
CONTENTS

CHAPTER 1

ANGRY BULL

The crowd roars as a bull and its rider dart out into the **arena**. The rider holds on as the bull jumps and **bucks**. Then he flies off the bull's back. The rider lands badly and hurts his leg. He cannot run to safety. The angry bull starts to **charge**.

A rodeo clown rushes in front of the bull. He shouts and throws his hat into the air. The animal bolts toward the rodeo clown. Others help the injured rider to safety. The rodeo clown jumps over a fence just before the bull gets to him. He has done his job!

CHAPTER 2

RODEO CLOWNS

Rodeo clowns protect bull riders from wild, angry bulls. Fallen riders are often in danger of being stomped or **gored**. Rodeo clowns distract the bulls. They make themselves targets so riders can get to safety.

Class Clown

Many rodeo clowns learn their skills at a rodeo school. They take classes on everything from bull riding to clowning around.

There are three main types of rodeo clowns. They often work together in teams. The main type of rodeo clown is the **bullfighter**. This clown is a skilled athlete who battles raging bulls. He is the primary protector.

One or two bullfighters stand at the edge of an arena. They are ready to rush in at any moment. They know just how to get a bull's attention. They run. They throw things. They shout. They do anything to distract the bull from the rider.

Golden Rules

Bullfighters follow two golden rules. Breaking them can get a rodeo clown hurt or killed.

#1 Never run in a straight line. It is harder for a bull to charge when a bullfighter runs in a zigzag pattern.

#2 Never run backward. It is easier to trip and be trampled when running backward.

Some rodeos include two more types of rodeo clowns. One is the **barrel man**. This rodeo clown hides inside a large barrel. He pops out to distract the bull. The barrel protects him. The other type is the **comedy clown**. His job is to entertain the audience.

Rodeo clowns wear loose clothing that tears easily if caught on the bull's horns. They also need plenty of protective gear. Most wear pads on their arms and legs. Vests protect the chest and ribs. Good padding can be the difference between life and death.

CHAPTER 3

DANGER!

Running in front of an angry bull is dangerous. Bulls weigh up to 2,000 pounds (900 kilograms). They can charge at more than 20 miles (32 kilometers) per hour. They easily **trample** rodeo clowns under their weight. Bulls can also knock people into the air. Many rodeo clowns suffer from **whiplash** when hit by a bull. Broken bones and **concussions** are other serious risks.

Rodeo clowns understand the dangers of the job. They know that bulls are strong and **unpredictable**. Still, they are willing to put themselves in harm's way to protect others. Rodeo bull riding could not exist without them!

Tragedy on the Job

In 2008, bullfighter Donny P. Martin tried to stop a bull that had destroyed a gate and escaped. The bull hit Donny with great force and sent him into the air. Donny landed hard on the ground. He suffered brain injuries that resulted in his death.

Glossary

arena—an open area surrounded by seats; arenas are used for public entertainment.

barrel man—a rodeo clown who hides inside a barrel and pops out to distract the bulls

bucks—lowers the head and kicks the hind legs up and out

bullfighter—a rodeo clown who is skilled at fighting bulls to protect fallen riders

charge—to rush forward to attack

comedy clown—a rodeo clown who entertains the audience

concussions—severe head injuries from hard blows

gored—pierced by tusks or horns

trample—to crush under one's feet

unpredictable—not always behaving in the same way

whiplash—a neck injury caused when a person's head is snapped back violently

To Learn More

AT THE LIBRARY

Hamilton, Sue L. *Rodeo*. Edina, Minn.: ABDO Pub. Co., 2010.

Kupperberg, Paul. *Rodeo Clowns*. New York, N.Y.: Rosen Pub. Group, 2005.

Reeves, Diane Lindsey. *Scary Jobs*. New York, N.Y.: Ferguson, 2009.

ON THE WEB

Learning more about rodeo clowns
is as easy as 1, 2, 3.

1. Go to www.factsurfer.com.

2. Enter "rodeo clowns" into the search box.

3. Click the "Surf" button and you will see a list of related Web sites.

With factsurfer.com, finding more information
is just a click away.

Index